CW01497155

JULIE McNEILL poet, author and v
creative writing workshops and
and supporting individuals with
Mission Dyslexia series and three .... is Poet-
in-Residence for St Mirren FC Charitable Foundation and the
Gaffer of The Hampden Collection. She has performed at various
literary events including Edinburgh International Book Festival,
Edinburgh Fringe, Limerick April is Poetry Series, Aye Write, Push
the Boat Out and StAnza International Poetry Festival. She is the
2025 Pauline Saul Writer-in-Residence with Kirkudbright Fringe.
Her poems have appeared in *Best Scottish Poems* collection 2023
and as poem of the week in *The Scotsman* newspaper.

By the same author:

Mission Dyslexia : find your superpower mind, be your brilliant self with Rossie Stone and Paul McNeill (Jessica Kingley Publishers, 2021)
Ragged Rainbows (Dreich Chapbooks, 2021)
Something Small (Drunk Muse Press, 2023)
We are Scottish Football (Luath Press, 2024)
A most unsuitable game: celebrating Scottish women's football fifty years after the ban, co-editor with Karen Fraser and Fiona Skillen (Tippermuir Books, 2024)
Part of Mission Dyslexia series with Rossie Stone and Paul McNeill:
Positivity with Persisto (Hachette/ Jessica Kingsley 2025)
Creativity with Creatia (Hachette/ Jessica Kingsley 2025)
Wellbeing with Willforce (Hachette/ Jessica Kingsley 2025)

From the library of

The Book Fairies

... to read and pass on...

PLACE FOUND	READER	DATE	THOUGHTS ON THE BOOK

#ibelieveinbookfairies www.ibelieveinbookfairies.com

Luath Press Limited

EDINBURGH

www.luath.co.uk

First published 2025

ISBN: 978-180425-236-9

Printed and bound by
Clays Ltd., Bungay

Typeset in 10.5 point Sabon by
Main Point Books, Edinburgh

To voyaging, in all its forms, and voyagers

Contents

*'The train went north, we went north,
love went north and across the sea'*

Trying to Remember

Abbotsford Bar, Rose Street

It's a museum piece, this place,
the Jacobean ceiling dripped in rich
reds and gold, a dark mahogany bar
solid as a Spanish ship, built in the
golden age of pubs. I've already got
a favourite table.

My eyes are fixed on a man alone
in the corner, he places his hands
this way, then that, slowly,
with purpose, like he's trying them
on. He looks in wonder at their
movement, their patterns and lines.

They're not new, though, I've seen
these hands before: as a girl I curled
my fingers around one thumb, reached
for them on walks, was surprised
when they folded my own small hand
in theirs. Affection was hard won.

He was always waiting at the window
when I visited. Even on days I tried
to surprise him, even in new windows
when he was too old to stay far away.
I thought you'd come today he'd say,
the sun was shining. Or, *the rains*

have brought you here. Must've been hard
for a man like that to wait for life. We
would sit in the smell of wax, petrol,
Brylcreem and grass in the shed. I'd
lean in to hear his stories of the road,
feel the walls shake with his wicked laugh.

When he died I dreamt of his hands
every night for a month: rough, shovelled,
worn, too big to hold delicate things. A life
mapped and etched into every rivet and scar.
I traced them when he opened his palms
long enough to let me in.

Trying to Remember

I'm sitting beside a big picture window
watching the sun set
over Bute, Arran, Cumbrae.

All evening the light has been
throwing shadows. The orange
glow, the miracle of the flat tide

the boats cooried in for the night.
Ferries have chugged like taxis
from the early hours.

Did you ever catch one? There's so much
I don't know. The new coastal path
is awash with benches,

a rainbow assortment
of resting spots every few steps,
looking out to sea

and I know that this is where
I would have found you:
two hands on the crook of your stick

staring out half-blind,
the chorus of seabirds enough
to drown out your thoughts.

Things are smaller than I remember:
the steps up to your front door,
the swing park, the distance

from your house to the place
where we heard the fairies laugh.
How did you end up here

in this west coast village so far
from home? I like to think
it was the sea

stretching out, the chatter of gulls
or that heron
as it wrestled an eel, but maybe

you got stuck, a penance,
and you washed up back in the tide
to a place you were trying hard to leave.

Missing

The half-light and promise
of sun seeps in
through the crack in the curtains

the streets have been singing
for days. I want to show you
the things I've seen:

that futuristic train,
the small dog in a bag
and the cool beer on every table.

I thought I saw you in that cafe
with the small birds
your tired face illuminated

by the sun, the Imperial Castle
behind, and last night
by the river

the moon was so clear and bright
I was moved to tears when
I reached for your hand.

Mary from Murroe

walked barefoot to school
though she didn't need to,
hid her shoes in a bush
near the cottage

padding rough soled with the others.
Mary is not buried here
in the graveyards
with ruined chapels

and daffodils surrounded by kin:
Ketts, Hickeys, Collins'
she couldn't leave her children
built a life across the sea.

Mary I remember the rosary beads
draped across your hands the day you died
the purple necklace I bought you
still around your neck

and your laughter, even when you
lost all your words
bar cabbage and home. Even when
you shrunk in the hospital bed.

Sometimes I lose you in the story
of our life, Mary, but as I grow
I see your love
was never something you made me work for.

Now I'm standing at your cottage door.
Nobody is home
the coal sack is overflowing round the back
and I see the whole long miracle of you.

The things you left,
the things you built.

Waking up in Dún Laoghaire

Light floods the room
Rosin is cooking sausages
and the red and blue
boats bob softly in
Dublin bay.

I slept soundly stretched
out on the polka dot bed
in this strangers' house
dreaming of the men
or ghosts

who in their own ways
brought me here;
and the open-armed
women who welcomed
me home.

Ordinary Things

The bus from Fairlie to Largs
was my favourite trip. I know
my siblings jostled for beds
in the house but in my memory
it's always just me and you.

I never gave a thought
to what the others might have been doing.
As far as I was concerned I'd got
the prize. There on the bus
free as your carer, there to be your eyes.

Always some small job to be done.
A stamp at the post office,
a small package needing dropped,
a mooch round the Sally Army shop
for suits worn by dead men.

The *candy store* always just before
the ride home: slabs of fudge
and quarters of rhubarb and custard
to hide from squawking gulls
and sisters. You didn't loiter

as I scurried along in your wake
like a seabird, greedy for crumbs.

Pipe Smoke

Carcinogenic coils swirl into the dreich morning air
brushing across leaves turning from green to auburn
wrapping their tendrils around park benches
hanging like haar

I tasted you there in the park that morning
just as I was losing sight of you. I swallowed
the memory of Murroe, of peat stoked fires
and my first sips of the amber nectar.

I leaned closer to the coils, an apparition
on my morning commute, and lingered
so as to take another gulp of you. I would
have stayed there all day

but my stubborn feet carried me back
and on.
I think I'll take the long way home
and see if you are waiting for me there.

Silence

Carve the runes and be content with silence –
George Mackay Brown

No more music now,
not a note shall flow
from that small house at Yesnabay
just south of Skara Brae,

a silence now at Sandwick
tucked in and bedded down
amidst the coastal cliffs
bricks built up like sea stacks

a shelter there in Stromness
from wind-crashed waves
from the rugged, wild, enchanting
and the impossible to tame.

A pause, here
for stories,
for humour
and for drams.

As birds of every colour
circle overhead, words wash
and rush like rapids
through our reeling heads

as we do our best
to content ourselves
with silence.

Ring of Sea and Shell

The way the band flexes
and curves around my finger
to keep the stone facing up

how you hook yourself
to other rings: the heart-shaped
one my daughter bought me,

my grandmother's wedding ring.
That soft swirl of gold
against smooth marble white

you are the Eye of the Sea
or the Heart, I don't recall.
I remember the day you

were gifted to me after an absence
in a soft gauze bag,
almost apologetically

You don't have to wear it
I remember easing it
onto my finger

like the right foot
slipping into a glass slipper
and admiring you

in the brilliant afternoon
light. I could've seen
the sunset, stood ankle-deep

in warm waves
as I wondered
what was ever there before.

Easy

It was easy love
easy for him
and I was greedy for it:

I was smart, I was pretty
I was his favourite.
I knew how they felt about him

how they had been left
and let down by him.
I knew she had the suitcase

packed under her bed
and yet I kept
writing his story:

over and over
I wrote him big,
brave, accomplished.

One for the road, another
his hands, his voice.
Now I'm standing

at your door
in the village
where your eyes first flashed

upon him. It is hanging
off the hinges, gaping wide
like an empty mouth,

the damp coal sprawls out
from the sack on the stoop
and spills stories,

which pour down on me like rain.
Suddenly, I see you
at fourteen keeping house

sailing across the sea
being buried
by your children,

the ones you reared.
I see the love
that wasn't easy –

easy for him,
perhaps
not for you.

Birthing

Novices

He's cutting his teeth
on the ropes
keeping his guard up.

I can see the fear
in his shoulders,
in the tap, tap, tap of his foot.

I've reached for his hand
many times on the paths
we've trodden together.

When they announce
his name to a packed crowd,
I watch him walk into the ring.

I see what this is,
all it means and now
I am the one who is afraid.

I don't want this
to be something else
he has to recover from.

When the bell rings '
I watch him grow again
those fourteen years

in a millisecond
and know he doesn't need
my hand on his back.

He tightens his own grip
surprises fear by running
head first towards it.

Birthing

After Young Mother in Grotto, Rodin

I watch you sleep beside me
a nightmare brought you here
but you settle quickly in my arms:
mouth half open in soft exhale,
brown hair fanned out on my pillow.
Your porcelain skin glows in the half light
like a saint.

I think of the years I prayed for this,
the times I lost you in a single line
test or in the uninvited red reminders
too early, or worse, late enough
to instil that old brute hope.

I remember long, black nights spent
padding the cold kitchen floor
with you swaddled softly, fighting
every inch of sleep, wrestling
through the loneliness of dawn.

Birthing is an open wound, exposed
and raw in a world you're too good for.
I want to hold you in my body, drip feed
you just the honey, drink the poison
to keep it from your lips.

Raising Boys

Your green felt tip,
the back of a school
letter and that familiar
pattern: boxes for
goals, a centre circle
and that impassioned
explanation of positions
and possibilities.

These windows are small,
soon you will lose your
enthusiasm for these
fantasies and I will
teach you about injustice.
Your phone will tempt you
to follow Andrew Tate,
to turn a blind eye to suffering,

to feel you are not enough.
Is any one of us enough?
I look with sadness at this
picture of my son
fresh faced and undeterred:
he believed so strongly
that the world was good.

Wrapped Up

I'm walking my daughter to school,
she is still young enough to want
to hold my hand and delights in
teaching me about Minecraft.

She tells me she's made a training ground
in the virtual world so that I can persuade
the other mums to join me there
and *I will be one step ahead.*

She's a walking cotton ball
with jacket and mittens of powder puff blue
and, honestly, it's a wrench
to let go of her hand

half way through her earnest
explanations of Obsidian and Endermen
but it's time for school
and time for work so off she goes.

The cleaners and dinner school staff
chat on their morning break about which
children they slip an extra portion to-
'it's a sin' they say, affectionately

and I settle for these small slices
served on hot plates
and at school gates
to start my day, nourished.

Midweek Mornings

On week days
he wakes screaming
breathless

I coax him through
the steps:
not too big, tiptoes really

half-spoons of cereal
his school uniform
on the radiator

to take the cold edges
off. His toothbrush
placed carefully

at the right angle.
One foot in the shower,
two, pants, trousers,

I do the tie
pausing after each step
to hold him

as he crumples
into my neck.
I colour code his day

stack books neatly
in plastic wallets
ease him, ease him away.

Bella, Bella

On Saturdays we swim
then a long walk
through the park, a train ride
and four tube stops to donuts
and chats in Greggs.

Bella barely takes a breath:
scanning subway passes
shadowing squirrels bouncing
from tree to tree,
her arms straining skywards.

She talks animatedly
about the new boy in her class
who doesn't speak English,
and how she will learn Ukrainian
on her phone so they can be friends.

Bella offers her subway seat
to a man with a toddler
and I see right then
the woman she will be.
Alfred waits for her

outside the bakery,
wrapped in a greying yellow
sleeping bag.
He knows her by name,
Bella, he smiles

as she presses a shiny coin
or two into his palm,
wishes him a *happy day*.
She saves half a yum-yum
in her swimming bag

because *dad likes them too*
and through all this
I ache for her,
wonder how to keep
Bella, pure Bella.

Washing Cars in Storm Babet

My son is washing cars
in his half term.
When everyone else
flew south for warmth,
when bins were sailing down
the street and rain
lashed at the pebble dash
he started washing cars
with his pal.

He pushes his soft hands
into warm suds, reaches
on tip toes to shine the roof
of the silver 4x4 three streets
down while curtains twitch,
sizing him up. His shoulders
are learning how to carry
dejection as he knocks twenty
doors of no, for every yes.

He's discovering, too, that
people can be kind: the woman
at number 73 tells him there
should be more like him,
gifted him a bucket. The old
guy at the corner thinks
it's a disgrace how few jobs
are about for boys his age,
slips him a fiver.

He washes until it's dark or
he's rigid with cold or his friend
has to go to judo. He's got
grand plans for the gold coins
in his pockets: a bumper Christmas,
Dubai, pancakes for tea.
He's washing cars in a storm
while his pals try Mad Dog
and trade vapes in the woods.

He's trying to move
I know from small boy
to young man, dabbling
in jobs and vices, pushing
out and away.
I hope they open doors
for him
if he knocks again
tomorrow.

Hot Chocolate

It has rained for days,
as I move my clothes
out this room, now yours,

the patch on the ceiling
is darkening. You tell me
you've had 'the talk',

that the girls gathered
afterwards in the toilets
and agreed a code word

if their period started
at school. *We're going
to ask for hot chocolate*

you laugh. I think
of the men I've escaped
from, gossip I've shared,

tampons borrowed, given.
Tests that have been
taken, confessions made

of all kinds, the tears
and youth I've shed in toilets.
The boys are traumatised

after handling a sanitary pad
of course. They add it to things
they will never discuss in toilets.

Here's Your Jotters

To the teacher
who took my son's golden jotter
in her bony hand and guffawed
at the size of the margins,

ridiculed the back-to-front G's,
made his errant full stops an example
I bequeath one day in a room
where everyone gets the joke but you.

To the Brexit voting gammons
I bequeath half an upside down
Wetherspoons pie, crustless
with soggy edges
for every special occasion

and a blue passport
you'll never use.
To the bore-a-fuck boyfriend
who gave me glandular fever

three weeks before my GCSEs
I bequeath you
a lifetime of polite nods
at your shite conversation

To the *stop the boats* crew
I bequeath you compassion,
try it on
it might look good on you.

And to those who
told me not to study philosophy
because it'll never lead
to a meaningful job

I bequeath you
lives, unexamined.

Electric Light

It was less floodlight
more searchlight:
a fifty foot tower
and a single beam

following the ball.
Players left stumbling
in darkness or suddenly
blinded, the lamp

too fast, too slow,
off the pace.

My son plays every evening
in the glow of the security light:
the grass is a muddy bog,
posts lean to the left

and the scarecrow goalie
has lost a gloved hand.
The light shines too bright
then off, then bright again.

I see his beautiful face,
strobed and weather beaten
determined to play the game.
It doesn't occur to me

to tell him to wait
for the daylight to come back.

Mind's Eye

In each child's bedroom
a plant: impulse bought
like vitamin pills or
history books to
ease the guilt of
imperfectly mothering.

Beauty and oxygen
to remind them
they are loved. I read
today that some people
cannot see pictures in their
mind's eye:

their children, an apple,
the sea. They see only
what's in front of them.
It's Easter Sunday
and the sun warms
my face over breakfast.

I see the bright buds
forming on each small
plant, my swollen
belly and that first
spring where everything
brimmed with wonder
at your arrival.

The garden needs tended,
we will have to remember
to water the plants
but your first over-confident
steps in dandelion
and fresh grass return
to me as easily as
that day you fell into my arms.

Something Small

In all honesty I feared
she'd never get there
'h' and 'b' and 'p' and 'd'
'6' and '9' 'dash' and 'line'
yesterday is tomorrow and
a month could be a year,
for her.

The shape that her mouth makes
when trying to sound them out
the extra breath
of thinking time, catching herself
and closing it for fear of a mistake.

But yesterday she laid them out
like a rainbow,
arced and beautiful, she engaged
the left and right
shouted the sounds as she pulled
the letters down from A to Z so easily.

Something small
but not so very small,
at all.

Sweet Pea

I don't know why we called you Sweet Pea
probably because having you was sweet
and you were about the size of a pea.

You were about the size of a pea
when we joked about calling you Rocky
and marvelled at my growing belly.

How can it swell so much when you
are only the size of a pea? I think I maybe
wore my maternity clothes too soon.

You were about the size of a pea
when we made announcements to expectant
grandparents and laughed as they said, 'about time'.

When you grew to the size of an apple
the sonographer left the room for a second opinion,
I don't think she needed the second opinion,

cold jelly on swelling belly, I was exposed.
we could see it, though. One heart, not two
mine, not yours.

In springtime I planted sweet peas in the garden
but I couldn't find you there.

Blood

He wraps his hands for a fight:
binds them over and over
gum shield fitted in his mouth
like a horse's bit

and I think of you telling me
of how you became men.
barefoot in trailer parks
and scrubs of land

with hands bound like this:
taut, tight
and your hair and heart
as wild as Rannoch.

Sometimes blood calls to blood
I think, whether pulsing under lengths
of cloth like this, or migrating
towards a wound, to heal.

Beautiful

After Maggie Smith Good Bones

He's fourteen and pushing it, later
and later, the circle widens to pals
and parts I'm unfamiliar. Is it safe son?

Aye I think so mum. The wee one sees
too much: weighs the plastic in the ocean,
counts the bombs, knows the animals

she couldn't save today. Tunes in
too intently the news. You're safe
little one. You sure about that mum?

Maggie Smith wrote a poem
about Good Bones, it starts
life is short but I keep that from my children.

Life is short but I keep that from my children.
Today they followed the path of a stingray
across the aquarium floor, climbed a hill

with wind on their face and laughed easily.
The little one saved a beetle
stuck on its back and her brother

took a step back from the edge.
I thought: *this place is beautiful*
You two could make this place beautiful, right?

Love Goes North

Going Home

I'm on a train that stretches
the length of central station
snaking through familiar land:
the forests my father tended
the hills where rain
whipped my face as a child

my carriage is barely occupied
and I've chanced a table
beside the huge window
draped with blue sky,
trees that look like arrows and church spires
that keep my head tilted up.

I'm running away again
between this place and that,
I've bounced this path for years
this time, though, I go towards love,
an old love, and an old home
and it struck me

that my favourite thing
about choosing a home
is how easy it is to leave
I'll pull that loose thread
another day. For now,
the light is on my face,

my heart is flighty and I'm
on a train again, taking me back.

Anster Sea Wall

I don't know how long you have been standing
or how many times they put you back together -
you have pieces which look the wrong way round,
or upside down, your veneer has peeled away
exposing all your mechanics and, honestly, it
doesn't look that well thought through.

You are not like a jigsaw at all: one brick sits
uneasily next to its neighbour, there are gaps
everywhere more like a small child's fort
all precarious and avant garde. Your photo
is in the bar up the lane in black and white,
you holding back the sea the last line of defence

all those pieces and gaps somehow enough
against the full force of the waves. I saw you do
this last night in the semi darkness from my window
and felt myself brace with you each time the waves
rushed in. Yet there you stood all evening, confident
in your place until the cowed water retreated.

Tomorrow I will walk to the beach, plant my feet
in the sand dig my toes into its depths hold myself
strong in your shadow and brace for the incoming tide.

A Rainy Night in Soho

whisky and I only dance
at Christmas time

there, she wraps me in smoke
and holds my throat to the fire.

The Pogues are telling me
not to sing of the future

and *not to dream about
the past,* and I think

I'll take their advice:
this taste, the heat,

that familiar curl
in my gut.

It has been a year filled with
pain and miracles again,

I've stopped trying
to make sense of it

I just turn the music up
and pour myself another glass.

The Slow Train

I'm on the slow train:
Gretna, Dumfries, Barrhead
the light is liquid
between mist and cloud
over Annan where the third day
of the hen do sesh rolls on
in this two carriage tin can.

I have left the warmth and madness
of old friends who have scattered
into the distance.
Another year of news: deaths,
births, misery and survival
my heart aches
with the ease of them

as this train pulses north.
I hug a scarf to my chest
for comfort and think
of the miracle of these
souls, not the pain
of leaving so much behind.

No Scotland No Party

In the Allianz arena
tears flow unexpectedly
as Flower of Scotland reverberates
around this coliseum

I cannae believe we are here
I pull my teenage boy in close
and my heart near bursts.

Three minutes into the game
and an hour after the opening show
two girls announce their arrival

'scuse me, cheers pal
Danke, danke shoen
danke-shoen thank-yer-son

she shouts in my face
affectionately
as she passes my boy
small kilts, saltire faces

and two plastic Proseccos
in each hand balanced perfectly.
As they settle in, apply lippy
take a selfie air kissing each other

in a puff of raspberry scented vapes
Germany score their second
Linda is FaceTiming Shaz who
lives in Coatbridge saying

'That place would be nothing without you hen
The heart of the whole company
They'd be fucked without you'

Stand up if you hate England

rings out. She stands. Sits.
Then stands.
Oh fuck I'm confused.
If I stand do I like them?

The two girls clap along to every chant –
German or Scottish – disnae matter
They make Scott Mctominay fit any melody
On FaceTime they shout loudly

about who the hell would take off
John McGinn and stick on Billy Gilmour?
When Scotland score, one is at the bar
the other on the phone

which is catapulted in the air
like an overhead kick
time seems to slow
as it somehow lands perfectly
on the lap of her red kilt.

Gooooooaaaaalllll

The Germans sing in unison
cheer rhythmically, chant like monks
score five goals, are impenetrable

but as we all know
there's no Scotland no party

Love at Central Station

in the chill
of Central Station
his hands glide
easily over
the keys
of the piano

I can't describe
the feeling
adequately: the point
at which
I realise he is there,
the melody,
the way my chest
lightens.

I am smiling,
as if meeting
an old friend.
It feels something
very close to love:
this stranger
this place
this music

I see him deftly
alter
the rhythm
of the day
unconscious
foot tapping,

changes of pace
straightening of backs

the soundtrack
of welcomes
and goodbyes.
He doesn't look
up, his grey hood
is pulled tight
like a monk

he has no need
for audience
or applause.
Yes, it
all feels
something very
close to love.

Refuge

Sometimes drowning doesn't
look like drowning, head tilted
skywards, hands waving
it can look a lot like living.

Across the vastness of oceans,
forests, deserts, bricks and mortar
sometimes home is not a place.
It is your hands holding me

in the half-light, or my own
tracing the lines of your face
before dawn. Refuge was
a white cliff, an open embrace

a place to make something
beautiful, again. Refuge is my
own hands pulling me
out of the depths to the shore.

Rail Replacement

Outside central station
it's all police cars
and rail replacement buses

the pavements are slippy
and the young ones
leap and squawk

between pubs. Rain
has been dribbling
down windows all morning

but I am full of fire.
The Christmas lights,
the afternoon drinks

that phantom itch that
needs scratching. We
are on top of the world here

as we hang like stars
above the station,
and it's still a long way home

Connection

When I saw you cry
for the first time
I thought about that boy
in our school
seeing his first snow,
soft white flakes
floating past the window.

The teacher took us outside
to let him feel the cold
on his tongue and eyelashes.
He made a snowball
tried out the arm movements
to leave an angel in his wake.

When I saw you cry
I could not press
the parts to heal you
but there was a softness
and a kind of grace:
like that day in the snow
pure and impossible to forget.

Trying to Find Joy in January

I choose the long walk, the one
meandering the Forth and Clyde
canal, stretching to the bridge
at Torrance where fresh saplings
rise from mulch. I walk with you

and your plucky dog In her purple
coat who rolls in everything. We
wade through bog-drenched fields
and gift each other the *hard to hear*,
scraping away the veneer, stomping out

our disappointments in the mud
holding each other. I find fun
in falling, slipping, catching the gate.
Solidarity in talking and I don't have
to tinsel-coat a bit of it.

What a rare thing this is, in the
shiny-matching-PJs,
too-feart-to-put-the-heating-on
health-kick-hell,
how-many-days-to-payday-anyway
just fields and fields of real.

All Eyes on Glasgow

A picture hangs
in *The Scotia Bar*
where I contentedly
marinade: an old train
station packed tight
with shadowy figures.

Soused in cheap lager
and sepia tones
I am frozen in it. Signs
for *Capstan cigarettes*
and *Johnnie Walker*
fight for centre stage

but it's the journey
that holds me. There's
aye sadness on the platform,
folk leaving, being carried
away, but on the day
I boarded the train north

from Carlisle to Glasgow
seventeen years young
whistles echoing in my ears
I didn't turn my face back,
not even for a moment,
to check if anything was lost.

Green

wide-eyed
with the kind of green
that made her a target
she travelled north
in borrowed clothes

unaware of the borders
she was violating
mouth full of
butterflies and fresh
starts. The first time

an Orange Walk boomed
past her Maryhill flat
window she leaned out
all joyful-like thinking
it was a pipe band

cheering the men trying
to break the drum skin
at the Pape church's door
cheering as the crucifix
burned into her neck

cheering the green gills
curling and shedding
onto the floor leaving
her soft underbelly
dangerously exposed.

Mill Grown

for the Anchor Mill girls, Paisley

This wasn't Paisley, this was another place
a place for scheming meet-ups in the lavvy
where you could get a full head hair dye

ear piecing, big Cathy's six inch beehive
and the perfect brows on your lunch break.
It echoed with shouts fae the avon wummin

- *get the orders in!* The cotton girls drifting past
with soft snow in their hair. This was a place
with its own language: signs of 'T' for tea

lip reading above the din. We spilled
out of scheme buses, packed to the rafters
out onto the Mile End Bridge where

we threaded our way through to Friday.
Pay packets cracked, our feet thundered back
and straight up the toon for hair lacquer top-ups

and American tan tights for the dancin.
There was a boom, and we were the start
of the thread. Connections spanning the globe

but none so bold as here, where we sewed new
sisters and fashioned fresh families into our town
within a town where we were all mill-grown.

Queen Street Station Piano

People mill like ants
rushing from one feast to the next
as he plays the piano
in Glasgow's Queen Street Station.

Today he wears a black waterproof jacket
a small rucksack flung at his feet
yesterday he was a retired woman
in a red sweater, the day before a teenage boy.

I love that music is found here
in the dirt and squash and rush of the station
it reverberates above the hiss of trains
and whoops from the Lycra-clad festival kids.

I walk in slow motion to my train
in time to the melody. Everything that's
happening happens now in my peripheral vision:
leaving is just the bit before meeting again.

Glasgow, My First Love

Autumn has settled
on Glasgow's sandstone.
The sky is a brilliant blue
clouds in soft vapour trails
tickling the tips of chimneys
and flagpoles

Underfoot the pavements
have been washed and shine
with early morning rain
as men in Glengarry hats
and half-kilts stumble their way
out of the dark

My city is gleaming:
the first lights of Christmas
wink from every bar, the
auburn crisp of hedgerows
warming our chests,
and that sky: Saltire blue
and pure white, I am in love.

Toil

The world is divided into folk
who care about plastering walls
and folk who don't:

my pal has spent four months
tripping over her children
to peel back forty years

of white paint, to painstakingly
brush her banisters white again
but – smoother – she tells me

she'll know it's been done right.
Another friend says that knowing she
will die soon is a sort of freedom,

that her last scan indicated
she might have longer
and she worried she'd have to

start sweating the small stuff
again. What a fucking inconvenience
she laughed. In the end

everything is at the mercy
of the elements, small doors
and windows in the slate

make us imagine otherwise, but
really it'll all be left on hillsides
or scraps of land, in ruins

The Street Preachers

One ear each we bend together.
Track number four of the Holy Bible:
She is suffering

I watched, as you rose to meet me
alone, headphones on, your
shuffled steps made sand
of the generations-old stone

Track number five: *Archives of Pain*
your key is in the bin; you don't fit in;
you suck at gym. Your trainers have four stripes,
not three; you still pray before your tea;
Tammy girl and Lambrini meets crochet and iced tea.

You can't breathe. You're counting.
The minutes. Until. Five. Past. Three.
As you fell to track eleven, I believe
I wonder if the music faltered, or played on:
Die in the summertime

Below the Blue Mountains

I used to dig for worms:
fingers rooting in the damp earth,
my knees mosaic- prints of grass
and sharp stones.

I shovelled and dangled
these worms gleefully
by hand or stick
from place to place:

made them follow luminous bugs
across a leaf span,
watch the hairs on a beetle's leg
prick upwards.

We learned together
what an ant looks like
when its jealous or afraid;
chased squirrels up the staircase of branches

to the tips of trees.
In the dark of the den
I would hunker down
beside the hole in the hedge

and open our mud cafe:
passing pies, coffee, pine kernels,
daisy chains
through the hawthorn.

Here in the heather scrub, dry-mouthed,
the blue mountains have
never looked more pleasing,
I feel them pull me up and on to the summit.

Instead, I squat down
beside the gorse bush as if in prayer
at the foot of these great gods;
scratch my nails into the dry earth

press my ear flat to the soil
searching for a wriggle,
a scurry, a portal.

Botox

I facetime my friend
but the face that answers
is not my friend's.
The forehead is frozen
the lips are bulging
and she needs to actually
tell me she's crying
as her face can't do that
on its own anymore.
The eyes are red
but the rest is all pulled tight
around the truth
I'm laughing
at her alien head
and the disconnect
between the sound
and the sight of her.
She's crying because
her next door neighbour
one half of the
through-the-fence covid bar
is moving away
she's taking it all personal.
Now she's laughing
at me laughing
and the wine is flowing
and I've woken up the bairns
and pieces of her crack
though the sheen
and she'll see the neighbour
for lunch sometimes

and she tells me
my face looks a lot more haggard
through a screen
and that really
I should think about
a little Botox.

Botchergate

police van corralled
discount store laden
no place for a nice girl

you
were my childhood
playground

outward chaos raised hands
in-sync with teenage angst
as we stumbled through

weaving by chip wrappers, blades,
and those fowk fae Maryport
down for *The Fightin.*

Top Stop hot scraps served
by perfect Peter: the usual –
gravy on a soft bap

saved the next day from being
a total toilet-bowl-hugging disaster
kept us coddled

in the inevitable taxi queue
sing-along/ domestic/ romance.
Your neon lights drew me in

like a moth, singeing my wings
every Saturday but leaving me
counting hours for another go.

Of course I was young
so healed quickly.
You were never boring:

belly-laugh, sore cheeked stories
stretching us through to adulthood.
You cradled six teenage girls

together, stretched your arms
around our young shoulders
then placed a soft hand on our backs
at kicking out time.

Love Goes North and Across the Sea

Maybe it's the wine: two large glasses
of Cotes de Provence, or the mussels
submerged in a perfect
shallot and thick cream broth.

I watch the sea stretching out
through the window
– flat and wide – as the last of the
sun licks its ripples and waves.

As the huge hulking ferry arrives
from Barra or Mull
they winch the gangplank
into place. The restaurant empties

around me and I need to say
so many things, but the words
feel too small in my throat
so I tell myself I'm happy,

'so happy to be here' I say
and I am. On this beautiful night,
in this life, with the sun lighting
the picture window I drink it all in

Shame Must Change Sides

Girls Eating an Ice Lolly by a Crumbling Wall

She stands in front
of the crumbling wall
hand on hip,

serious, no smile,
a bright orange
ice lolly raised

to her face.
A strange incongruity,
a taste of somewhere

else. In some ways
she could be
my beloved girl, looks

about the same age,
tousled hair falling
loosely on her shoulders

standing in the mid
afternoon beside pieces
of stone. One, our

decaying garage,
the other what's left
of her school.

They both contemplate
their next moves:
my open faced girl

follows a Palestinian
poet on Instagram,
asks me how writing a poem

can land you in jail.
The other follows the
vague curve left

by the rubble road,
trying to find
something still steady.

Pressure

When he asks if we're feeling the pressure,
the answer is we've felt it all our lives.

Just the right amount to squeeze a pal's hand when she is breaking,
to cup a daughter's face and tell her she's more than good enough.

The extra hours burning the midnight oil to prove you're just
as smart as them
and to then get up and burn the oil again.

The pressure in your legs when you drive hard towards the goal
determined you will earn your place as the team's one and only girl

The pressure to look, or feel, or be as they'd expect.
Nothing more and nothing less.

So when he asks if we're feeling the pressure
of a nation on our backs,
our answer is 'Aye'
but we girls know a thing or two about that.

Are you #ThatGuy?

I've been the only woman
squashed between feather and armpit
on the Mount Florida train
on match day:

You on the right train love?

I've kept my mouth shut
at games not wanting to draw
too much attention
even when I've had plenty to say,
like

Why don't you shut the fuck up?

I've pulled my son
and my daughter's hats down
around their heads to block out
the noise.

She'd get it, she'd definitely get it!

I know the statistics:
the crunch of dejection
stamping up the driveway
the rattle of the key in the door

silence.

My daughter will soon be too old
for me to clap my hands
over her ears, my son
now sits with the Young Team

too cool to wear his hat,
all his senses open
to the world, laughter
is his overcoat now.

I should've called it out
when their wide eyes
looked to me for answers.
This year

it took that politician
over six minutes
to read out the names
of the dead.

Destiny

For Wendy Wood 1892–1981

You often quipped, *if I was born
in a stable, would you call me a horse?*
A proud daughter of Scotland
like me, by choice not birth.

You hung your name on a long
line of sculptors, those who
carved beauty from lumps
of clay, no wonder you could

see the potential in this land.
Rumour has it you marched to
Bannockburn tore down the
Union Jack and hung a Lion Rampant

in its place. When they carved
your stone, it was with a single
worded epitaph – a patriot,
Gwendoline.

Home rule hunger still seeps
across this weary land. We hear your
call, though, to tear down, to build,
to realise our destiny.

Zero Sum Game

Glasgow transforms,
is a zombie apocalypse
a dystopian wasteland

on these days even
the green grass hisses
at the blueness of the sky.

The distant horizon wears
its red like blood and everyone
retreats, or organises.

The small weans in the nursery
part like oil
and water.

They only use the blue
or the green plastic forks,
metal cars, paints, playdoh.

They drink out of blue water
cups or suck from green
cartons. Blue befriends Blue.

Green embraces Itself
in the mirror. When they
go home in green cars

to green houses or on
blue bikes scooping adults
spilling out of blue pubs

they learn the flute or the fiddle,
worship the Tricolour or Union Jack.
March or pull the curtains tight.

Non football fans mark '*Old Firm Day*'
on calendars with a large X
the way doors were branded

to ward off evil spirits.
They hoard their supplies
the day, the week, before

so they don't need to venture
into the streets, cut their path
through the fog of fear and hate.

A people's sport
for the people's good? Four lads
had a dream? Let it be

a nil-nil draw, everyone stay safely
in their corners
for this zero sum game.

The Morning Bus to Portobello

'Can you sign our petition
to stop the war in Gaza?
Can you sign our petition
for a ceasefire?'

This woman who could be my mother
is crying now:
she's been here all day
watching people pass,

hearing them say
'Leave them to their war'
'Let them kill each other'
'Free the hostages'.

As I sign she tells me
her daughter is a nurse,
that she's got four grandchildren,
and asks *'why isn't there outrage?*

Why don't people care?'
'I know', I say, put
my hand on her arm.
It's 10.30 in the morning

outside Waverley station and
we are both weeping.
As I board my bus
she gives me a sticky

Palestinian date
'for emotional energy'
wipes tears from her cheeks.
I chew the sweet fruit

watch her, through the window.
The people swarm by
but she is still the loudest
voice in the street

Shame Must Change Sides

I've seen them outside of hospitals
with placards and piety
making young girls feel like shit
on the worst days of their life.

I've seen them lurk in courtrooms
analysing how much she'd had to drink
or how the guy was a promising athlete
or did charity work at the weekends.

I've seen them at the school gates
sniggering in Lycra
she's at home all day that one
she's always at her work

she's got above her station
no ambition, no drive
her hairs a bloody riot
it's like she's not even trying

Gisele didn't chose to be a rallying point
she didn't chose to be raped
she did chose bring her face into the light
and to say 'I'm not ashamed'.

Permanent Red

The day is a permanent red
each spring bud carefully
wrapped in Dante's cardigan

the sunlight slices its way
into your bedroom
but you wake up grey,

enough white to momentarily
imagine the simplicity of breakfast
then it slips to black.

I remember those times
the colours poured
down the sky like rain:

we drank too much
you shocked your hair crimson
and insulted all the right folk

before showing us up
with your love for this life
which treated you so cruelly.

This year spring is insipid:
laughter is lilac, muted,
and the days begin to purple too,
like a bruise.

I place yellow roses on your
windowsill like the ribbons
in that tree,
guiding you all the way home.

Future

Of course I want
all the big things:
equality and parity,
and a decline in celebrity
particularly those ones
who are famous
for being famous
aye those ones,
you know the ones I mean.

World peace
and kids who have enough to eat
without having to shame
those supposed to lead
with social media feeds.

Free speech
and the right to a roof
over your head and your own bed
in a place you can feel safe in.

Forget flying cars
and trips to Mars, extendable arms
or robots to clean your cars
I would take holding you
in my arms. Never having to look
at you through a screen again.

I'd take dinner parties;
pubs; film nights;
Christmas; dates;
crap dates; ceilidhs;
even funerals.

My wish? My wish is for
a future filled
with all the past I didn't touch
or feel, or breathe in
in a the way I would've done
or should've done
if I could've seen
the future.

War

There are too many moments
that we forget
that there is a war

that bombs and shells
and the dead fall
elsewhere.

My son asks
if he will be put on a train
if he will be sent to a camp

if he will have to wear a star
and leave us
I say to him no

not today
not yet
not us.

Level Playing Field

If it's not the huge green pole
it's the stewards' head,
and if not them
the barrier on the goal side,
or the opposition fans'
backs when they jump up

to applaud, or furiously vent
their rage. The only way
to know who has scored
is by lugging in
to the noise from the other end,
or ours. Don't think

of cheering, though,
or placing head
in hands in despair,
instead stare straight ahead,
stay mute
like the *vegetable* some
think you are.

Always
an afterthought. Any reaction
might earn you a bottle
flung furiously
at you, the closest
sitting duck.

For in every respect
you have entered
hell in a handcart,
you've been wheeled
behind enemy lines
and instead of that coat

drawn up against the cold
 or your teams' jersey
proudly put on,
you might as well have worn
a target
on your back

she is too young to die

when we walk
on the first day
of this new year,
her plucky dog
chases all the
good looking
joggers like
a dolphin
surfing the
bow wave
we spot a heron,
a kingfisher!

The cool canal
glows in
the half light
as we hover just
a smidge
too long
outside the gate
of that bloke
from Outlander
and imagine
sharing a dram
in his perfect
kitchen

we swap
stories
of raising teenage
boys: should
we still be tying
their ties?
She wonders
quietly
who will do them
when she is gone.
When she is gone.

Lost in Sleep

Cold

Dunlop
is a witches
cauldron.
From my seat
on the ice train

rain spits
through grey fog
rising from hollows
which I imagine
conceal

a network of
underground
worlds.
There's nothing
on this earth
colder I think

than the train
jutting north
jutting north.

Kintsugi

My friend gave me
a small saki bowl
when she returned to me
from a year in Japan

it was a fierce azure blue
with golden veins
I used to run my fingers
over them as they reflected

the sunlight. It sat on the
window ledge of my tenth
story flat and revelled in
looking completely out of place.

It was too exquisite to be there,
should've been the centre piece
in a museum or up in Park Circus
in a bay window at the very least.

You ask if I know Kintsugi
and I don't think about that bowl at all.
I hold my fingers to the thrum
in my veins and feel the heat rise

up my neck. The air catches
and feels heavy: once
I didn't notice it at all. I didn't see
the cracks before but now they are
golden.

Tender

After the blackened cod
crumbled and melted
into their mouths
with the large Pinot Noir
he took her hands

held them softly in the centre
then with thumb and forefinger
pressed the fingertips
firmly in turn:
one, two, three.

Such intimacy in these
moments shared in corners
in plain sight, thighs touching
under tables or a light brush
of fingers down her arm.

Under the Same Sky

Above the still of the sound
the cloud's open mouth
breathes fire

in another place
the sun sets in a crescent
as the band tunes up

for the evening
five hundred miles away
from the flat, black

sky I walk under
with my daughter:
her mittened hand

nestled in mine,
the same bright stars
above us.

Off Balance

I long to run for the hills
feel the sharpness of the
fresh air filling me.

I want to climb high
enough to feel small
or nothing or greatness.

I am there with you
through the brush
of bracken, searching

for the right notes on the
wind, my own foot slips
as the ground gives way

and throws you off balance.
I, too, am looking out
to the horizon

over the bright glare
of coloured lights
flashing like stop signs

over empty wine glasses,
the slow monotony
of puzzles, Lego, slime,

and in time the sun rises
achingly slow
transforming the palette

burning a path through
whisps of low cloud
bringing me rest.

Lost in Sleep

The moon is high
and bright tonight
you are far away

but I see you clearly
hands crossing
your chest,

holding yourself
tenderly
in sleep

your face is younger
pure, sweet
soft on the pillow

you are content
in dreams,
you're safe there.

I stretch my fingers
place them to my heart
feather light

close enough
to guess
that you're real.

Some Poets Get all the Luck

Sleep brings me gifts of
dark pubs, wine
longing and baggage.

Sometimes so much baggage
it takes all night to gather it
and my arms ache

as I wrestle it through
until morning. You are
in the Gardens of Versailles

guided by the Sun King
in paper costumes
paying homage

to the God of Light,
possibly a haunting thrown in
for good measure.

Even in dreams
you're so much better at this.

Wave and Sky

Building slowly, the dark
slick of water pushes up
until it touches the sky.

The muscular, blue-black
mists white at cloud tip
reach like hairs on the back

of my neck sensing danger,
or pleasure. It kisses the cloud
a slow caress of wave, water and air

in an alchemy of senses then,
it curves like an arched spine,
opens its mouth and falls, folding

into itself with a crash. Over
and over this miracle must happen
in nights and half lights, across

the vastness of oceans. The sun
dances on the edge of this perfection
as the sea swallows the wave, lies back.

Madras Mornings

For Leela

On this Madras morning
I find myself combing
for your prayer card
the one you gifted me
in Saint Andrews before
searing burnt orange
into Highland clay

I reach for your books
signed on my shelf
your laugh: *well*
everybody likes a
good murder
scroll your Twitter
and find your last
post is one encouraging
me, and the one
before that, the same
and it leaves me bereft.

I don't know where
to put your kindness
where to keep it now.
A self-assured woman
with so much left
to say. I will write for
you because what else
can we do
but chisel away

fold up your words
your warmth
and let them
weave their way
with mine.

Lunch

They are tipping
cold oysters down
their throats,
swallowing hard like
they're drowning.

He curls thumb
and forefinger round
the stem
of a large Malbec
and lifts it to his half-slack
mouth, gulps,

places it back
on the table. Her knee
presses against his.
I don't know the mystery of
who they are or
how we crossed paths

like this
but as I look on,
I know that this doesn't
feel much like lunch.
Everything here
tastes salty, tastes new.

Words

words that land
so beautifully
on the swell
of the Esk

or written
on the last bus
through inhospitable
countryside,

are packed carefully
into a poet's bag
with the croissants,
cheese pies,

badges, and
that mysterious
cloth. They fly
to a rooftop

bathed
in the light
of a Mediterranean
sunset,

where
the Acropolis
peers over
their shoulder

and a companion
reads joyfully
about the loss
of hope.

The words
are given away
in bars, on trains
at festivals

like they're
nothing at all,
or everything

we have
to mark this,
their miraculous journey.

The Mouth of the Wood

There's something about
the way the light falls
in this picture:
luminous green leaves

shine unnaturally bright
they are dancing
softly in and out of the sun's rays,
the way they, and I, did

every fine day I ran away
as a child. The edges
of the path are deep red,
bleeding into dark blue

at the heart of the wood,
just as I remember it looked
when my small sandshoes
stumbled defiantly over twigs

and pine cones,
the balls of my feet wincing
through thin rubber soles.
It pulls at a latent fear: I have

the same relationship
with the mouth of the woods
as I do with the depths
of the sea. The compulsion

of a small girl
strangled in coils of branches,
consumed by waves,
both lost, and at peace.

Sound

The ferry hovers
just above the rise
and chop of the grey sea

from Oban to Craignure.
Behind, the light is ethereal:
hills are sugared with snow

and ahead of us, a rainbow
passengers rush into
the wind to capture it.

I stay here: the sun
strokes my face
as sleet turns to rain

on the window pane
and Duart castle appears
flexing the muscle of Mull.

This morning I watched
the seasons change
through a wall of glass:

the dark rumble of snow,
the sheet of rain
and the light

caressing the waves
as she stretches
for the shore

Cherry Blossom

What I would give
to hold memories like this
sealed under domes of glass.

Nobody could say
it didn't happen or
it was somewhere else,

or another time. It would
be a specimen
to be dissected lovingly at will.

I know I'm pulled
to pink blossom. I feel lighter
when it falls like snow,

carpets the ground. If I
concentrate hard enough
I can feel the give of petals,

the type
I pressed into perfume
with my sister,

or see the
perfect bouquet
my daughter picked,

her face as warm as
the unending summer
she first arrived.

It's colder now,
the seasons
have changed:

brown leaves
under serious shoes
so I'll shelve that day

next to the blossom tree
where I put things loved,
things lost to the air.

Acknowledgements

'Pipe Smoke', 'Sweet Pea', 'Botox' and 'Something Small' were published in *Something Small* (Drunk Muse Press 2023)

'War' was published in *Best Scottish Poems* anthology (Scottish Poetry Library 2023)

'Future' was runner up in Bold Types Competition for Glasgow Women's Library 2021 and published online.

'Birthing' won the Burrell Collection Hidden Gems Poetry Competition 2024

'Kintsugi' was first published by Atrium online 2024

'Electric Light', 'Zero Sum Game', 'Pressure', 'Are You That Guy' and 'Level Playing Field' previously appeared in *We Are Scottish Football* (Luath 2024)

'Hot Chocolate' was published in January 2024 by Poetry Scotland

'No Scotland No Party' was published in *Keep Left* (Luath 2025)

Also published by **LUATH PRESS**

We Are Scottish Football

Julie McNeill
with photography by Campbell Ramage
ISBN 978-1-80425-157-7 PBK £7.99

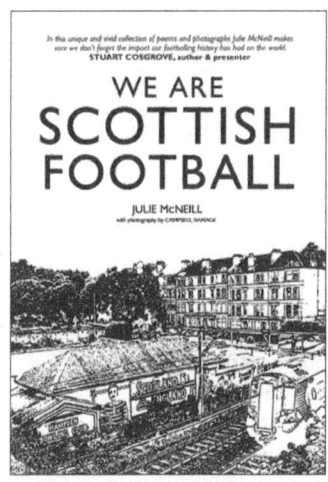

With a pen dipped in passion, McNeill explores the emotional landscape of football, bringing to life the highs and lows, triumphs and tribulations that define the beautiful game in Scotland. Her verses transport readers to the electric atmosphere of packed stadiums, where every cheer and roar reverberates through the pages. With eloquence and insight, *We Are Scottish Football* stands as a poetic tribute, capturing the soul-stirring drama and unwavering devotion that make Scottish football an enduring and enchanting spectacle.

A must read for any fan of football, history, poetry and Scotland.—IAN MAXWELL, CEO SFA

Details of this and other books published by Luath Press can be found at:

www.luath.co.uk

Luath Press Limited

committed to publishing well written books worth reading

LUATH PRESS takes its name from Robert Burns, whose little collie Luath (*Gael.*, swift or nimble) tripped up Jean Armour at a wedding and gave him the chance to speak to the woman who was to be his wife and the abiding love of his life. Burns called one of the 'Twa Dogs' Luath after Cuchullin's hunting dog in Ossian's *Fingal*. Luath Press was established in 1981 in the heart of Burns country, and is now based a few steps up the road from Burns' first lodgings on Edinburgh's Royal Mile. Luath offers you distinctive writing with a hint of unexpected pleasures.

Most bookshops in the UK, the US, Canada, Australia, New Zealand and parts of Europe, either carry our books in stock or can order them for you. To order direct from us, please send a £sterling cheque, postal order, international money order or your credit card details (number, address of cardholder and expiry date) to us at the address below. Please add post and packing as follows: UK – £1.00 per delivery address; overseas surface mail – £2.50 per delivery address; overseas airmail – £3.50 for the first book to each delivery address, plus £1.00 for each additional book by airmail to the same address. If your order is a gift, we will happily enclose your card or message at no extra charge.

Luath Press Limited
543/2 Castlehill
The Royal Mile
Edinburgh EH1 2ND
Scotland
Telephone: 0131 225 4326 (24 hours)
Email: sales@luath.co.uk
Website: www.luath.co.uk